FLORIDA WILDLIFE
CORRIDOR EXPEDITION

FLORIDA · WILDLIFE · CORRIDOR

EXISTING · PROTECTED · AREA
CORRIDOR · VISION

M I L E S
0   25   50   75   100

Painting by Mike Reagan

FLORIDA WILDLIFE CORRIDOR EXPEDITION

EVERGLADES TO OKEFENOKEE | 1000 MILES IN 100 DAYS

Photographs by Carlton Ward Jr

Essays by Mallory Lykes Dimmitt,
Joe Guthrie & Elam Stoltzfus

COMPASS EDITIONS

Compass Editions
Tampa, Florida
info@compasseditions.com

ISBN 978-0-9826396-2-7
Library of Congress Control Number: 2013901938
First printing, March 2013

Editor: Carlton Ward Jr
Contributors: Mallory Lykes Dimmitt, Joe Guthrie, Elam Stoltzfus
Designer: Hannah Dillard

All photographs, unless otherwise noted, by Carlton Ward Jr / CarltonWard.com.

Printed in the United States of America.

Learn more about the Florida Wildlife Corridor at FloridaWildlifeCorridor.org.

To visionaries who laid the stepping stones that this expedition could follow, friends who made the journey possible and everyone committed to keeping the heart of Florida connected.

40°26'47"N 79°58'36"W Ocala National Forest

TABLE OF CONTENTS

FLORIDA WILDLIFE CORRIDOR EXPEDITION

Over the past two centuries, natural Florida has been fragmented into smaller and smaller pieces. Conservationists have protected important places like Everglades National Park, Ocala National Forest, Lake Kissimmee State Park and hundreds of smaller reserves. Over time, these natural areas are becoming islands, surrounded by development and increasingly isolated from one another. As a result, native wildlife face the prospect of extinction while regional water supplies continue to be depleted and degraded. The solution to these problems is protecting and reconnecting, wherever possible, the natural corridors that are the foundation of life for us all.

The Florida Wildlife Corridor is a collaborative vision to connect an ecological corridor throughout the length of Florida by protecting contiguous natural lands, waters, working ranches and farms. Florida Wildlife Corridor goals include:

- Protect and restore habitat and migration corridors essential for the survival of Florida's diverse wildlife, including wide-ranging panthers, black bears and other native species

- Restore water flow to the Everglades and sustain water supply to southern Florida

- Continue to safeguard the St. Johns and Suwannee Rivers and water supply for central and north Florida

- Sustain the food production, economies and cultural heritage of working ranches, farms and timberlands

- Bolster local economies through increased hunting, fishing, birdwatching and other forms of tourism

- Give wildlife, plants and people room to adapt to a changing climate and sea level rise

- Engage greater numbers of people, especially youth, to connect with natural Florida

The Florida Wildlife Corridor Expedition, led by photographer Carlton Ward Jr, conservationist Mallory Lykes Dimmitt, biologist Joe Guthrie and filmmaker Elam Stoltzfus, was a 100-day, 1000-mile trek that explored the last remaining natural corridor through the length of the Florida peninsula. Traveling only by their own power —paddling, mountain biking and hiking (plus two days on horseback)—the team entered the backcountry of Everglades National Park on January 17, 2012 and emerged from the Okefenokee National Wildlife Refuge on April 25. Their purpose was to raise awareness that a natural corridor through the state still exists and that we still have a chance to keep it wild and connected. The expedition calls attention to places where road building, development and intensification of agriculture have reduced natural habitat connections to a few fragile threads that could be forever lost without immediate measures to protect them.

In the following pages, you will meet the expedition team, learn about their inspirations, and join them on an epic journey of exploration and discovery. Starting in the Everglades, you will paddle the mangrove coast and river of grass, traverse big cypress country, explore the Everglades headwaters, navigate the St. Johns River, trek through Ocala forests and springs and immerse yourself in Osceola National Forest, the Suwannee River and the Okefenokee Swamp.

25°19'13" N 81°4'23" W Flamingo, Everglades National Park

INSPIRATIONS
by Carlton Ward Jr

The ferns spread thick around the trunks of subtropical hardwoods that deeply shade the forest floor. The ground is wet beneath my feet, quieting slow and deliberate steps. Joe Guthrie stalks 10 yards ahead but is nearly out of sight through the dense foliage. He motions for me to hold back—a good sign—he's caught a bear.

A few minutes later, he threads a syringe to the end of a jab pole and edges within range to sedate the animal. Anchored to a maple tree by a single cable snare, the bear is very much awake. Joe describes the radius around the tree as the "circle of death," a good reason for his stealthy approach. Hunter and spear deliver the drugs and the bear settles by the base of the tree. Black and wet with mud, the bear stares at me through penetrating amber eyes that embody the heart of wildness, a depth of life every bit as ancient and visceral as the growl of a jaguar in the Amazon or the ground-rumbling charge of a forest elephant in the Congo.

This bear's forest happens to be on a central Florida cattle ranch only two miles from U.S. Highway 27. It feels like a rainforest in the summer heat. The canopy of bay trees interspersed with maple, cypress and pine hides much of the light—and also the fact that civilization is so near.

The bear is a 195-pound, two-year-old male that Joe and his colleagues have named "M13." The animal awakens wearing a GPS tracking collar that will help them understand how bears are traversing the patchwork of natural, agricultural and developed lands of the Northern Everglades—a water drainage basin spanning from the edge of Orlando south to Lake Okeechobee.

It is 2006, my second year documenting Florida cattle ranches and the same month that the cover story of *Florida Trend* magazine is headlined: "Final Frontier: Growth is coming to Florida's heartland. Who gets to say where it goes and how?" Inside the magazine, the article reveals plans for two new highways that would crisscross the Northern Everglades—M13's home range. There is lengthy discussion of transportation, evacuation and development corridors, but no mention of corridors for water and wildlife.

I begin wondering: If we're having a public debate about building concrete corridors, shouldn't Floridians be talking about protecting ecological corridors at the same time? I go to the Internet and search for "wildlife corridors" in Florida. There are almost no returns. I know scientists and conservationists had been advocating the importance of ecological corridors for decades and that big projects like the Ocala to Osceola Corridor (O2O) have been achieving impressive results [I would later learn that O2O is one part of a plan for a statewide network of corridors].

27°5'44" N 81°17'40" W Carlton Ward Jr sits with "M13" as the sedative wears off (photo by Joe Guthrie).

But it appears that the importance of landscape connections has yet to gain widespread recognition. Wanting to see that change, I reserve the web domain FloridaWildlifeCorridor.com without fully understanding the scope of the adventure that is about to begin.

Carlton is an eighth generation Floridian who began his career photographing wildlife for the Smithsonian in Central and West Africa. He is now working as a conservation photographer, focused on celebrating and protecting Florida's natural and cultural heritage.

27°5'44" N 81°17'40" W Wet with mud and having just received a sedative, this 195-pound black bear "M13" will soon fall asleep and awake wearing a GPS tracking collar. His movements will help inform decisions about wildlife corridors.

CHAOS TO CLARITY

by Mallory Lykes Dimmitt

Today is controlled chaos. I'm at the grocery store in Homestead attempting to provision the Expedition, at this 11th hour, for the first leg of our 100-day, 1000-mile journey launching tomorrow. We've been planning this trek for a year and a half, and although the sense of urgency has hit, the rest feels surreal and not quite right. Is this how other high-profile expeditions begin? For starters, this Publix is not playing nice with the items on my list. Everything either comes in glass, not great for camping, or economy-size, not a good fit for the small food sacks we'll stuff into our kayaks. As I mull servings per package and make menu choices, I admit that I really only know one of the other three team members and I know very little about anyone's food preferences. My inner voice tells me that I should have insisted on practice trips together. As the team member with the most expedition experience, which is not saying much, I am well aware that the team dynamic is the most important thing to get right on a trip like this, followed closely by food. As I put my final items in the cart, I think, "here's to hoping that the others won't hate me after the first week, at least not because of my food choices." I've been in this store for two hours and I'm anxious to get back to the only vehicle in the parking lot with a sea kayak on the roof and finally steer to the Everglades, which are looming nearby but a world away.

Only, I'm not sure how to get there and the map on my phone won't load. There is one road to Flamingo, but finding it in this grid of sprawling 'New Florida' that

sits atop former Glades causes my blood pressure to rise, not an unfamiliar phenomenon for me when the people and vehicle density outnumber all of Western Colorado, where I now reside. I search the vehicle for a map of the paper variety—the first of many times on the expedition I will want or need a physical map over digital navigation. Reaching the "Robert Is Here" fruit stand, which signals that I'm going the right way, I stop for fresh local produce to augment the menu; limes will enhance the boxed, dehydrated Pad Thai. The milkshakes here are legendary.

Cruising the long entrance road through the National Park in the warm last light of day, I relax into the incredible scenery and the journey we're about to begin. Pacifying my concerns about our group of newbies in the Everglades backcountry, the temperature outside is glorious, the forecast is perfect and the tides are mostly going to be favorable (except for our longest day, par for the course).

My thoughts turn to gratitude for the conservationists who came before our modern day mission—the visionaries who had the foresight to protect the two immense wilderness complexes that bookend our Expedition, the Everglades and the Okefenokee. It's their groundwork that make this trek possible, and it's the refugia they protected (and the wildlife populations harbored within), that both anchor and necessitate the Florida Wildlife Corridor. Raising awareness about the habitat connectivity needs of Florida's native species and the health of our

26°52'9" N 81°36'21" W Mallory Lykes Dimmitt hikes through the northeastern corner of Babcock Ranch Preserve near the border with her family's Lykes Ranch.

watersheds is an honor, one that we owe to Ernest F. Coe, Marjory Stoneman Douglas, Harry S. Truman and Franklin D. Roosevelt. In remembrance of these founders and the Florida conservationists who followed, let the adventure begin.

Mallory is a seventh generation Floridian who grew up exploring the lands and waters of Florida. Those experiences shaped her love of the outdoors and the environment, fostering her career in natural resource conservation and policy.

27°54'53" N 81°21'17" W In the Everglades Headwaters, Tiger Creek winds between Tiger Lake and Lake Kissimmee.

TRACKING THE FLORIDA BLACK BEAR

by Joe Guthrie

When we caught him, M34 didn't seem remarkable for anything other than for being a black bear making a living in south-central Florida. He was 2 ½ years old, weighing less than 200 lbs. Wade Ulrey and I caught him on a patch of oak scrub in early October 2009, near the peak of the acorn harvest. On the morning of his first capture, we walked in silence toward the trap site, listening for the sound of a bear thrashing the brush, which would tell us we'd been successful. Our trap tree sat on top of a little scrubby knoll. In Florida, scrub habitats are usually dry due to their sandy soils and often the scrub will present what looks like an impenetrable barrier of stems and thorns. The understory around the single tall slash pine tree was a dense tangle of oaks, hickory, staggerbush and greenbriar. Because the scrub was so thick, we had to get within 15 yards of the tree before we could see M34 and gauge his size.

The scrub draws bears during the fall, and in a good year they may work the food-rich patches for months, gorging on scrub oak acorns, hickory nuts and palmetto fruit. During trapping season we use the fire lanes to search for fresh bear sign, so we knew a little about M34 and his movements before we caught him, from following his tracks in the sandy fire lanes. We could not yet imagine how important that unassuming young male would become to us.

At the time of M34's capture I was working as a research assistant in the University of Kentucky

Department of Forestry, living at Archbold Biological Station near Lake Placid, Florida. I migrated to Florida in 2004 to work on the project under Dave Maehr, professor of conservation biology at UK. Dave had a long history in Florida, having helped lead research efforts on the endangered Florida panther in the 1980s and 1990s. He left his agency job to pursue his doctorate at the University of Florida in 1994. An incredibly productive biologist and prolific author, he'd published almost 70 peer-reviewed articles by the time he returned to academia. During and after his years tracking panthers and bears, Dave was an outspoken advocate for the importance of private land in conservation efforts. He penned an article in 1990 that suggested the use of conservation easements as tools to ensure that wildlife corridors would remain in place in south and central Florida. Conservationists have long been portrayed as being at odds with the interests of private landowners. Dave worked very hard to gain trust and maintain good relationships with landowners and sportsmen not only because he cared about wildlife, but also because he thought of Florida ranchers as good land stewards, who prided themselves on the health of their wildlife.

Dave's mentor at UF was cut from similar cloth. Larry Harris was the author of one of the defining books for the nascent conservation biology discipline, *The Fragmented Forest*, published in 1984. Dr. Harris was an expert on reserve design, having helped design

25°37'54" N 80°43'14" W Joe Guthrie traverses the Shark River Slough in the backcountry of Everglades National Park.

parks and reserves in Africa and Texas. This affinity for landscape-scale conservation and biodiversity, along with a healthy irreverence for most things man-made (excepting fine liquor), brought Dave and Dr. Harris together. (essay continued on page 56)

(essay continued on page 56)

Joe Guthrie is a conservation biologist based at Archbold Biological Station in Venus, Florida. His graduate research focused on bear corridors and helped inspire the Florida Wildlife Corridor Expedition. He is now working with the National Wildlife Refuge Association to create new refuges and conservation areas throughout the Greater Everglades.

29°10'55" N 81°42'27" Ocala National Forest provides essential habitat for black bears and other wildlife. By protecting and restoring forested corridors, bear populations in south and central Florida can be genetically reconnected to populations in north Florida and southern Georgia.

OFF THE BEATEN TRAIL

by Elam Stoltzfus

For me, a filmmaker, the Florida Wildlife Corridor Expedition was a once-in-a-lifetime opportunity to showcase the landscapes, wildlife habitats, winding waterways and conservation legacies of Florida. Experiencing the wilds of Florida was like an epic dream come true. It is as Dr. E.O. Wilson says, "our love for nature is an innate and genetically determined affinity of human beings with the natural world," that explains my continual interest in exploring an in-depth connection with nature.

During the expedition, some of my favorite moments were early in the morning, especially on waterways with the fog rolling in. One particular memory: we were on a tree island in the Everglades and misty showers greeted the day, followed by the sun breaking through the rainy clouds with a rainbow appearing over the sawgrass horizon. I quickly set up the camera. The composition was right there, five feet from the tent. What a moment, being immersed in the scene developing around me.

Another magical memory was with a flock of roseate spoonbills along the St. Johns River. It was shallow enough that I could move the kayak with my toes, and I moved slowly through the marsh, keeping the camera mounted on the kayak steady. Finally I was within a few yards of the birds. To be able to capture these images is a gift.

Having the opportunity to listen to stories people shared during 90 video interviews and spending time with them in their home landscapes was like having a front row seat in a college class. For many, this was an investment into the greater cause of the corridor concept. A number of them walked with us, some kayaked, others rode horses along side with us. One of the greatest treasures of the whole experience is what people gave and shared and invested into the expedition. I'm so honored because that's what the journey is all about—those people and their stories.

At the end of the trek a journalist asked me: "Can you give a sentence summarizing the journey?" My immediate reply was, "into the wind, against the current and off the beaten trail." Certainly our journey was an arduous one, with long days and grueling terrain as we traversed Florida's remote heartland. It was filled with obstacles that we would not have overcome on our own. All throughout our journey, from the moment it was merely an idea, there have been people pushing it toward reality. From trail angels to pastors, from professors to teachers, from commanders to generals, from bear biologists to park rangers, from corporations to small businesses, from kids to parents, people of every walk of life have supported our quest.

As we experienced the corridor, we discovered what brings us together, what we have in common. We all want to protect natural Florida for current and future generations. We want to see habitat restoration, endangered species protection, agricultural

26°15'17" N 81°9'37" W Elam Stoltzfus wades through ferns in the addition lands of Big Cypress National Preserve.

production and cross-agency cooperation continue as part of Florida's landscape. Our journey has shown what is possible. With your continued support we all have the opportunity to bring the idea of the Florida Wildlife Corridor into reality. May our voices reach further as we share this story together.

Elam is an independent filmmaker based in north Florida. His award-winning films have aired nationally on PBS, including Big Cypress: Western Everglades and Kissimmee Basin: Northern Everglades.

27°13'53" N 81°27'53" W Elam Stoltzfus and Carlton Ward Jr trek through a palm hammock on Doyle Carlton's Roman III Ranch in an area near the headwaters of Fisheating Creek, recently protected by a conservation easement.

25°19'24" N 81°3'57" W Oyster Bay awaits along the Everglades Wilderness Waterway.

"Camped in the Everglades at the edge of Florida Bay, listening to dolphins hunt the shallows. An exhale and inhale with each breach, erupting water followed by fluttering fish across the surface. In a few hours we will slip into their world. The journey begins..."

– Carlton Ward Jr | Day 1

TAYLOR · WMA
MIAMI
TAMIAMI · TRAIL
EVERGLADES
N
SHARK · RIVER
TARPON BAY
FLORIDA · BAY
KEYS
FLORIDA

MANGROVE COAST & RIVER OF GRASS

The expedition begins in Everglades National Park at the edge of Florida Bay, travels among the mangrove islands of the Wilderness Waterway, continues up the Shark River into the open sawgrass of the Shark River Slough, explores tree islands north of the Tamiami Trail and traverses west along the southern edge of Big Cypress National Preserve.

25°37'8" N 80°40'52" W Beneath starlight, Carlton Ward Jr, Elam Stoltzfus and Joe Guthrie pole kayaks through the shallow Shark River Slough on their third night in the open sawgrass.

25°17'30" N 80°47'52" W Red mangrove trees, typically associated with salty coastlines, stand over sawgrass and needle rush where the freshwater from the Taylor Slough eases south toward Florida Bay.

25°12′52″ N 80°57′17″ W On the first day of the expedition, Joe Guthrie and Mallory Dimmitt traverse Whitewater Bay, pictured left in the distance.

"We get a late start, which allows us to paddle in the dark, and it is perfect conditions and beautiful light, and as the sun goes down and we are still paddling quietly, we snake our way in through this beautiful channel to South Joe River Chickee for the first night." – Mallory Lykes Dimmitt | Day 1

25°19′13″ N 81°4′23″ W Whitewater Bay

25°9'1" N 80°55'19" W With as few as 500 in South Florida, American crocodiles are endangered in the US, though populations are rebounding in recent years. This specimen was encountered on the first day of the expedition, sunning itself across mangrove roots in the Buttonwood Canal between Florida Bay and Coot Bay.

25°24'9" N 80°58'7" W A swamp lily blooms among mangroves along a branch of the Shark River just south of Tarpon Bay. The amount of salt in the water here varies throughout the year. In the rainy season, when water flows strongly from the Everglades, the water can be very fresh, becoming much more saline in the dry season.

"We arrived at the Oyster Bay chickee in short order. It was sheltered from the open bay by a narrow island of red mangrove trees. A juvenile yellow crowned night heron stalked sullenly across the elevated platform of the chickee as we drew near, and finally flew as our boats bumped the supports." – Joe Guthrie | Day 2

25°19'25" N 81°3'59" W Elevated "chickees" furnished by the National Park Service provide excellent camping platforms along the Wilderness Waterway portions of the Everglades backcountry. Mallory Dimmitt manages social media from her room with a view.

25°25'10" N 81°0'13" W The houseboat of John and Donna Buckley floats anchored in an alcove of Tarpon Bay near the Shark River outflow. The Buckleys are "the eyes and ears of the backcountry"—seasonal park volunteers for nearly 30 years who helped guide the expedition from the maze of mangroves into the "river of grass".

"Carlton and Joe have their tents on air mattresses on the sawgrass on about 18 inches of water. I wish you could see this! I'm sleeping up on the platform of the gauging station. What a view. It's mosquito-ville tonight. No cell or Internet yet. Tomorrow we will paddle on the airboat trail." – Elam Stoltzfus | Day 5

25°23'4" N 80°54'55" W Small red mangrove trees pepper the shallows downstream of the Shark River Slough and just upstream from Whitewater Bay. An ample supply of freshwater, which flows in wide sheets in this area, is essential for the health of the estuary.

25°45'21" N 80°45'57" W One of 350 bird species that occur in Everglades National Park, a great blue heron forages in a seasonal pond. The abundance of wading birds in the park has declined 90 percent since the 1930s. Conservation measures to restore natural water flow and increase nesting habitat should benefit these icons of the Everglades.

25°26'28" N 80°47'2" W One of 50 different reptile species living in Everglades National Park, a garter snake moves along the branches of a coco-plum tree at Mahogany Hammock, possibly hunting for tree frogs.

25°25'36" N 80°58'31" W Everglades National Park, shown here in Tarpon Bay, contains the largest contiguous protected stand of mangrove forest in the western hemisphere. An estimated 75 percent of the game fish and 90 percent of the commercial fish species in south Florida depend on the mangrove system during some part of their lives.

25°25'17" N 80°56'35" W The surface of Avocado Creek, left, a tributary of the Shark River, reflects roots and leaves of red mangroves across from the Canepatch campsite. The expedition team camped here during their last night in the mangroves, which provide nesting and feeding habitat for numerous bird species. Clockwise from top left: great blue heron, snowy egret, tricolored heron and anhinga in Everglades National Park.

"We've been in this open sea of beautiful sawgrass prairie for almost three days... the only thing I can really compare it to is like being on an open bay or out on a big, big lake, because it's horizon as far as you can see in all directions and open light and open air..." – *Carlton Ward Jr | Day 6*

25°27'10" N 80°53'47" W Deep in the heart of the Shark River Slough, Carlton Ward Jr, left, and Joe Guthrie travel by push-poling their kayaks through the shallow sawgrass. The Shark River Slough is the largest aquatic artery in the Everglades ecosystem and the primary source of water for Everglades National Park. Water from the slough drains into a web of mangrove-lined creeks, right, that converge to form the Shark River.

25°51'24" N 80°46'12" W Afternoon clouds move above sawgrass and lily pads as seen from a tree island (like the small clusters of trees on the horizon). The 672,000-acre Everglades/Francis S. Taylor Wildlife Management Area buffers Everglades National Park and Big Cypress National Preserve from intensive agriculture to the north and urban development to the east. The 1928 construction of the Tamiami Trail cut off the natural flow of water like a giant dam, starving the national park downstream and drowning tree islands to the north, resulting in a 70 percent reduction in their numbers since the 1940s. Currently, the flow is being restored by elevating several miles of the Tamiami Trail via new bridges. In addition to improving water supply to the park, reconnecting the watershed will restore tree islands, increasing foraging and nesting habitat for wading birds such as this white egret preening its breeding plumage.

"The black surface of the water and the big cumulus clouds catch the slant of the sun, and the green grasses shine in the afternoon light. The beauty of the surrounding marsh is nearly enough to distract us from the real importance to conservation and restoration of the Everglades that the tree island itself represents." – Joe Guthrie | Day 9

25°45'21" N 80°45'60" W White egret

25°54'23" N 81°20'38" W Open cattails and sawgrass in the Turner River Slough give way to palm islands and distant cypress domes in the southern reaches of Big Cypress National Preserve. These wetlands form the Turner River, which flows into the Gulf of Mexico near Everglades City.

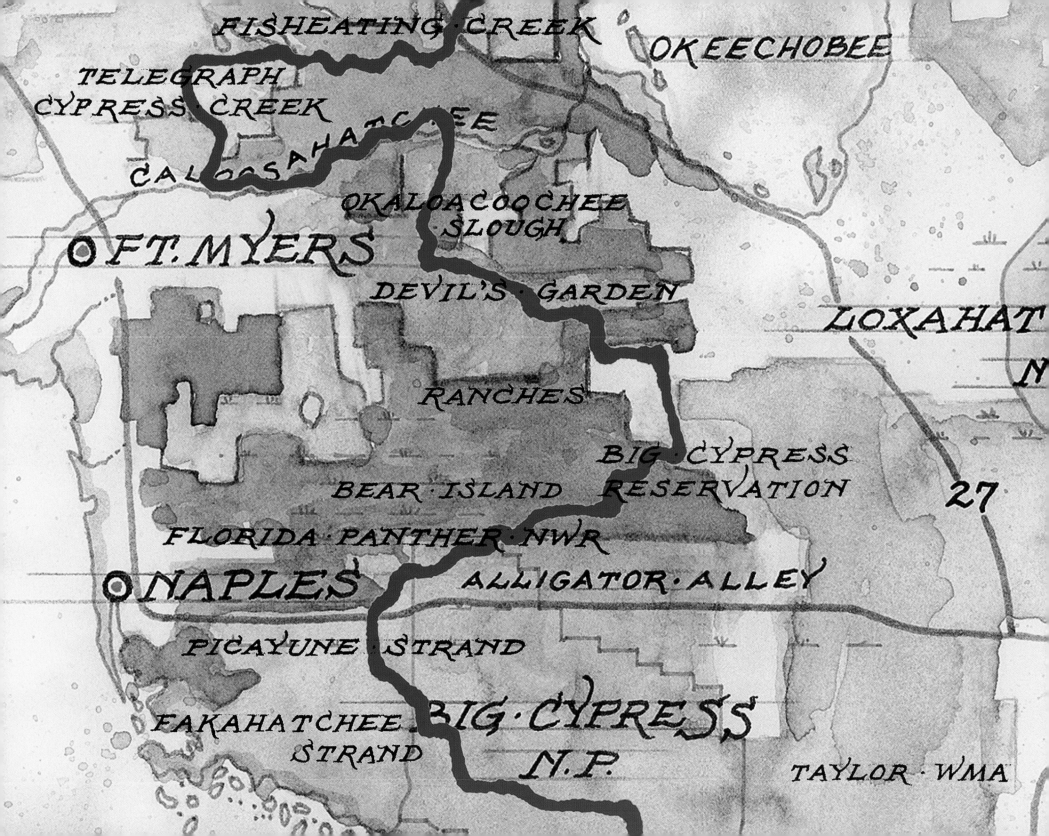

BIG CYPRESS COUNTRY

The expedition travels through Big Cypress country, including Big Cypress National Preserve, Fakahatchee Strand Preserve State Park, Picayune Strand State Forest, Florida Panther National Wildlife Refuge, Bear Island, Green Glades West, the Seminole Tribe's Big Cypress Reservation, cattle ranches around Devil's Garden, Okaloacoochee Slough State Forest, the Caloosahatchee River, Telegraph Cypress Creek and Babcock Ranch Preserve. These form the heart of Florida panther country and the Florida panther dispersal zone.

26°51′46″ N 81°42′48″ W A white egret wades among bald cypress trees in the 10,000-acre Telegraph Cypress Swamp. These waters drain into the Caloosahatchee River, Charlotte Harbor and the Gulf of Mexico. The swamp is now protected as part of the 73,000-acre Babcock Ranch Preserve, a cornerstone for the Florida Wildlife Corridor.

"We biked 43 miles west to the Fakahatchee Strand yesterday and are now waking up in an amazing flooded forest where our friends Clyde Butcher, Mike Owen and Renee Rau will join us for a day of swamp walking and photography. We are so lucky to be where we are and to have this opportunity. That places like this still exist in south Florida is a tribute to the work of many smart, visionary people going back many years."

– Elam Stoltzfus | Day 12

26°1'48" N 81°23'48" W Bright green bromeliads from the genus Guzmania hang from pond apple trees in Fakahatchee Strand Preserve State Park, which protects nearly 90,000 acres. The 22-mile-long swamp forest is three to five miles wide and connects its headwaters in Okaloacoochee Slough to Florida Bay. Florida panthers and black bears thrive in this important corridor.

26°1'47" N 81°23'47" W The long strap fern grows in wetland hammocks, often as an epiphyte hanging from trees as seen here in the Fakahatchee Strand. Backlighting reveals clusters of reproductive spores dotting one of the fronds. Its range in the United States is limited to southern Florida and Hawaii.

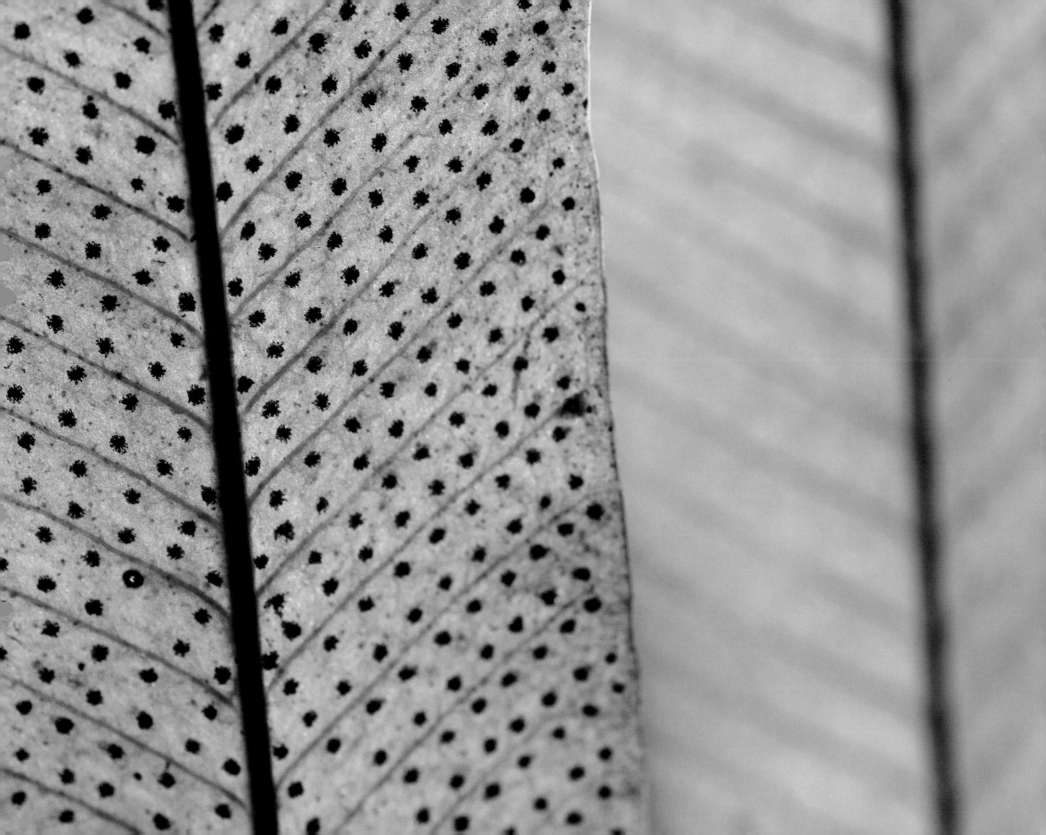

26°15′16″ N 81°9′16″ W Elam Stoltzfus, left, and Joe Guthrie wade through a cypress stand in the remote Bear Island region of Big Cypress National Preserve. Even in drier winter months, trekking from Florida Panther National Wildlife Refuge through this region entailed spending half of each day in knee-deep water.

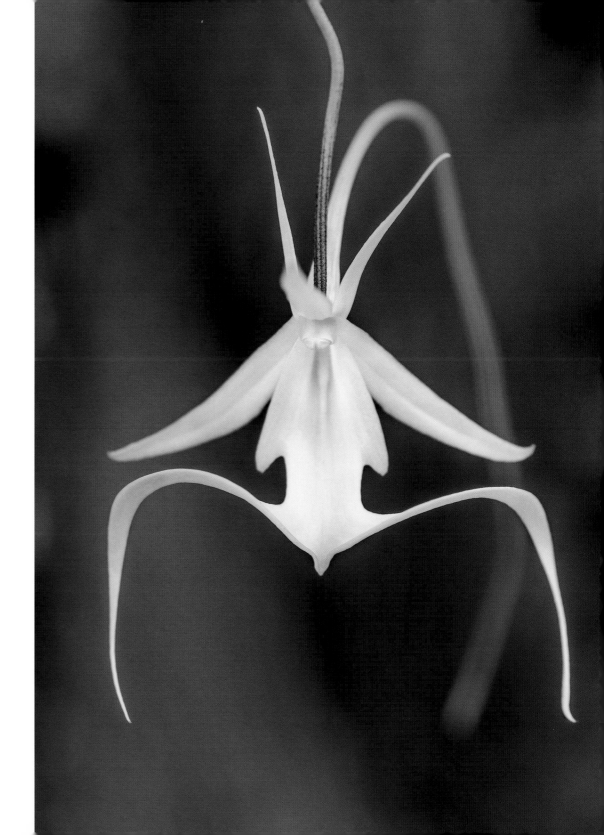

"Somewhere in the night I woke and heard a pair of barred owls calling back and forth from a tree above the camphouse clearing, slipping into their bizarre laughter, their silhouettes bobbing rhythmically toward each other in the branches. In the night it felt like a far corner of the world."

– Joe Guthrie | Day 13

25°57'5" N 81°21'36" W The rare ghost orchid spends most of its life as a nondescript brown plant, hardly distinguishable from a twig on the side of a pond apple or cypress tree. For a week each summer one in ten plants produce ephemeral white flowers that glow spirit-like against the dark swamps that shelter them. Approximately 2,000 ghost orchids live in south Florida, primarily deep in Big Cypress National Preserve and Fakahatchee Strand State Preserve, where this individual was photographed. Because orchid thievery could wipe out the population, the GPS coordinates listed are of a nearby ranger station.

26°11′41″ N 81°24′50″ W This yellow rat snake was found moving through sand and leaf litter in Florida Panther National Wildlife Refuge. It may have been hunting for small mammals or frogs which it would subdue by constriction. Skillful climbers, rat snakes also eat birds and eggs. This species is one of 31 snakes living in the region, only four of which are venomous.

25°59'16" N 81°18'14" W The sun rises over a wet prairie in Big Cypress National Preserve, which protects 729,000 acres of prime wildlife habitat at the core of the Florida panther population. The freshwaters of the vast swamps are essential for the health of the Everglades and the rich marine estuaries along Florida's southwest coast.

26°1'44" N 81°23'49" W The large and colorful lubber grasshopper is the most distinctive grasshopper in the southeastern United States. It grows to three inches in length and has small wings but cannot fly. Its primary food is leaves, which it finds in abundance here in the Fakahatchee Strand.

26°12'32" N 81°21'54" W A barred owl scans the forest floor from its cypress perch in Florida Panther National Wildlife Refuge. Moments after this photograph, this owl spread its four-foot wings and glided down through the trunks and branches to capture a small animal, which it carried to a more distant tree to eat. Barred owls prefer dense forests with large trees and relatively open understories.

26°52'26" N 81°43'24" W A Florida panther peers out of its fenced habitat at Babcock Ranch where it was used for education prior to the state purchasing the property. While wild panthers range through the same land, the majority of the population, estimated between 100 and 160, live south of the Caloosahatchee River. An individual panther can have a home range of 200 square miles, requiring it to cross numerous roads and properties. Wildlife underpasses are one way to protect panthers, other wildlife and people from deadly collisions.

"Feels like every 20 feet we're stopping to look at another print or another scat. We saw panther tracks and bear tracks and coyote tracks and bobcat tracks."

– Carlton Ward Jr | Day 16

26°9'13" N 81°28'2" W Clockwise from lower left: The expedition team crosses under I-75 between Picayune Strand State Forest and Florida Panther National Wildlife Refuge, led by Darrell Land (white shirt) and Kevin Godsea (tan) with Laurie Macdonald (purple), Brian Scheick (blue) and Elam Stoltzfus (orange). A panther crossing sign alerts drivers along US-29 between the panther refuge and Big Cypress National Preserve. An aerial view of the I-75 underpass through which the expedition traveled. A fresh panther track at Florida Panther National Wildlife Refuge (photo courtesy of Lisa Östberg).

"We love being on this property because it's a model for species diversity. It's an ecological jewel. And we feel like not enough people know it's here."

– Joe Guthrie | Day 18

26°16'8" N 81°8'34" W A female white-tailed deer runs through winter grasses at Alligator Ron Bergeron's Green Glades West. Adjacent to Big Cypress National Preserve, the private ranch protects some of the best wildlife habitat in the state, where both bears and panthers thrive.

26°15'51" N 81°8'58" W Bergeron met the expedition team at the edge of Big Cypress National Preserve and hosted them to ride across his property on horseback. From left to right: Kali Parrish, Clint Parrish, Ron Bergeron, Carlton Ward Jr, Elam Stoltzfus and Joe Guthrie (photo courtesy of Marie Bergeron).

26°18'12" N 81°0'46" W Morning fog clings to forest ridges at the Seminole Tribe of Florida's Big Cypress Reservation. The Seminole Indians trace their heritage to a great Creek chief named Cowkeeper who began raising Spanish cattle in the early 1700s. Driving a herd toward the pens, Michael Henry keeps that tradition alive. Ranching remains important to Seminole culture. Today the tribe is one of the top 10 producers of cattle in the United States.

26°31′13″ N 81°11′30″ W Cattle ranches provide important wildlife habitat and landscape linkages within the Florida Wildlife Corridor. Snuffy Smith helped the expedition traverse the 130,000-acre ALICO ranch in Hendry County, where he began working as a cowboy in 1974. ALICO previously sold 32,000 acres to create Okaloacoochee Slough State Forest and portions of their property are candidates for protection though future expansion of Florida Panther National Wildlife Refuge.

26°26′29″ N 81°3′20″ W Also in Hendry County, J Seven Ranch near Devil's Garden is part of a natural land corridor between the Okaloacoochee Slough and Big Cypress National Preserve. In fall of 2012, a group of whooping cranes migrated there from Wisconsin. The highly endangered species has recovered from only 22 birds in 1944 to nearly 500 birds today.

"It was beautiful paddling in. We could kind of tell when we had arrived at the preserve, just like a step back in time."

– Carlton Ward Jr | Day 26

26°42'58" N 81°34'29" W Elam Stoltzfus paddles the Caloosahatchee River at sunset. The expedition traveled downstream from the Florida panther dispersal zone near LaBelle toward Telegraph Cypress Creek and Babcock Ranch Preserve.

26°52'24" N 81°42'56" W An alligator floats motionless in a pond at Babcock Ranch Preserve. Panthers and bears utilize the property too. The expedition followed in the tracks of one black bear that traveled earlier from Babcock Ranch east through Fisheating Creek as part of a lengthy dispersal route that went as far north as Lakeland and the outskirts of Orlando.

"We meet the cattle crew who work the cattle on that 73,000 acre spread [Babcock Ranch Preserve]. They do the land management there to keep the pine forests healthy and the palmetto scrub healthy."

– Mallory Lykes Dimmitt | Day 30

26°43'51" N 81°20'0" W Palmetto prairies and pine flatwoods are abundant on cattle ranches throughout Big Cypress country and the Everglades Headwaters, as seen here in the Florida panther dispersal zone between the Okaloacoochee Slough and Caloosahatchee River. Cowboys like David Milburn, the cattle foreman at Babcock Ranch State Preserve, are often responsible for the land as well as their herds. In a unique approach for public land in Florida, ongoing agricultural operations including cattle and timber pay the full cost of land management of Babcock Ranch Preserve.

26°51'7" N 81°38'1" W David Milburn

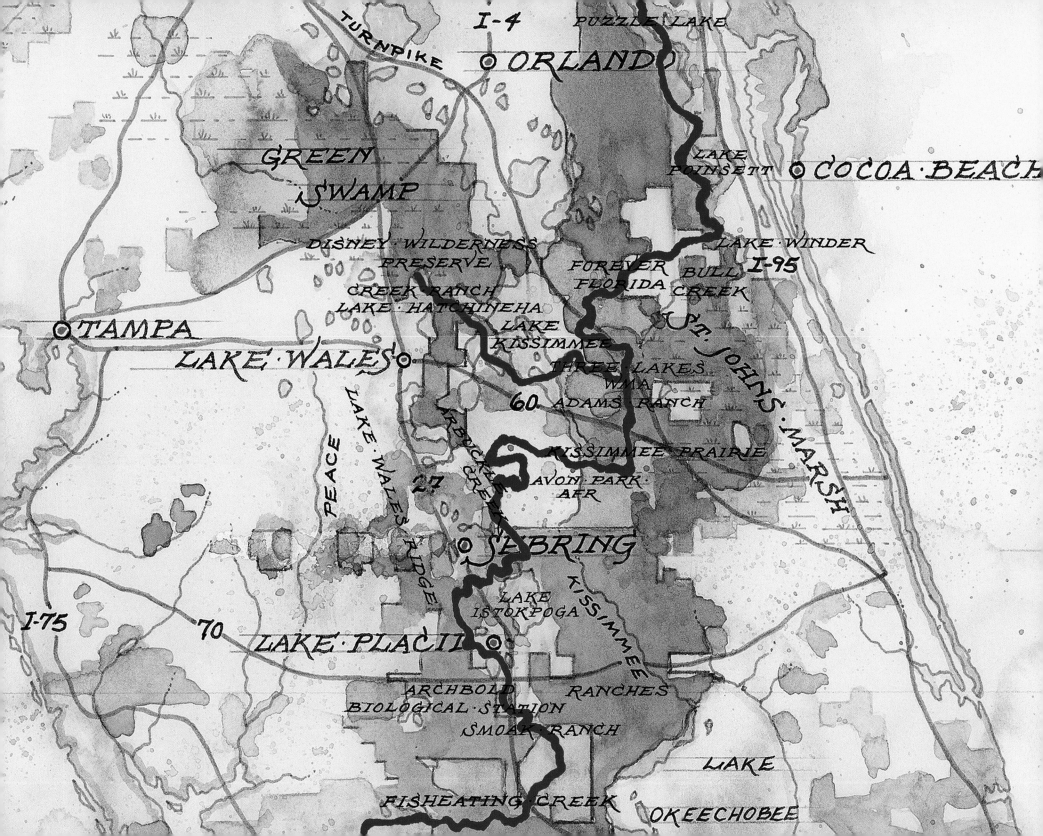

EVERGLADES HEADWATERS

The expedition enters Fisheating Creek in Glades County and paddles east toward Lake Okeechobee. After leaving boats in Palmdale, the team treks north into Highlands County, through the Lykes, Smoak and Hendrie ranches, Archbold Biological Station and new conservation easements on ranches in upper Fisheating Creek. They then paddleboard Josephine Creek to Lake Istokpoga, kayak up Arbuckle Creek to Rafter T Ranch, cross Avon Park Air Force Range, swim the Kissimmee River, walk Kissimmee Prairie Preserve State Park, mountain bike to the Adams Ranch and hike Three Lakes Wildlife Management Area. From there, they paddle Lake Kissimmee to Brahma Island and up to Lake Hatchineha before riding horseback from the Creek Ranch to The Nature Conservancy's Disney Wilderness Preserve.

27°52′12″ N 81°16′34″ W Joe Guthrie and Mallory Dimmitt lead an exploration in the Everglades Headwaters around Brahma Island in Lake Kissimmee. The tranquil conditions disguise the fact that the previous day's crossing presented 30-knot headwinds hurling giant waves—the most dangerous waters the team would endure.

"That next morning we started paddling a six-mile stretch of the Creek, from west to east, and it was kind of a half-paddle, half-walk, since we were dragging our kayaks some of the way because of the low water."

– Mallory Lykes Dimmitt | Day 29

26°57′19″ N 81°1′7″ W Spring clouds are reflected by Lake Okeechobee—the largest lake in Florida and the second largest entirely within the continental United States. Years of pollution have covered much of the sandy bottom with organic muck, which had been recently removed from the area in the photograph, restoring water quality and the abundance of fish and birdlife.

26°57′11″ N 81°23′28″ W The expedition enters the Everglades Headwaters via Fisheating Creek, using kayaks and standup paddleboards without fins to glide over the shallow sandbars.   Fisheating Creek is the only naturally flowing tributary to Lake Okeechobee, providing the second largest surface water source to the lake after the Kissimmee River.

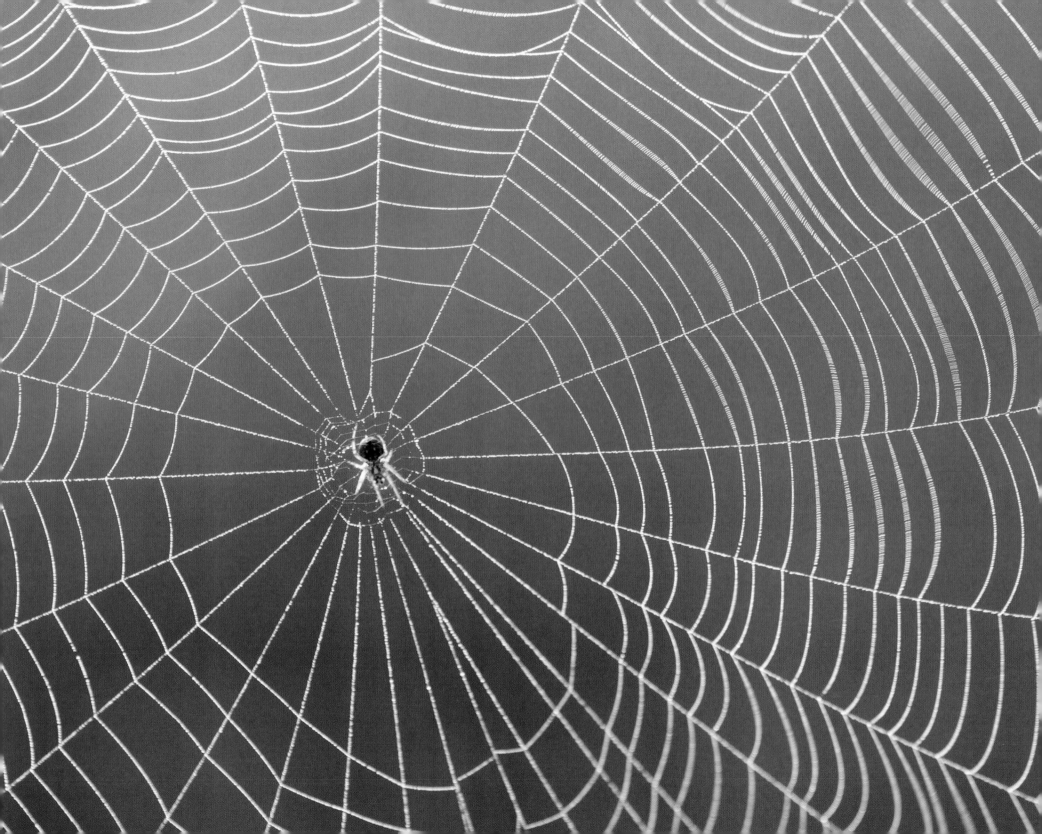

"This opportunity to combine the Florida Wildlife Corridor Expedition with crossing my family's land is a real treat."

— *Mallory Lykes Dimmitt | Day 30*

27°1'20" N 81°20'20" W A spiderweb catches morning dew on the Lykes Ranch, north of Fisheating Creek. The expedition traversed a portion of the Lykes Ranch that is protected via conservation easement. Conservation easements are important tools for habitat protection on private land, as are payments for ecosystem services. The route skirted a gopher tortoise mitigation site, where tortoises can be safely relocated to desirable habitat if their home range is in the path of development.

"The beginning part of the journey was on a lot of public lands—wildlife refuges and national parks. And this week has been mostly private lands. And that's been a great opportunity as well, because, as we look across the length of peninsular Florida, it is that matrix of land ownership and land protection opportunities that are really going to make this corridor."

– Mallory Lykes Dimmitt | Day 34

27°4'3" N 81°19'9" W Like the backbone of the peninsula, the Lake Wales Ridge rises from the surrounding flatlands west of Lake Okeechobee and continues north toward Orlando. Most of the original ridge has been covered by citrus or development. The remaining natural ridge offers some of the best wildlife habitat in the state, as seen on the Smoak Ranch, which is protected by a conservation easement and supports an important population of black bears.

27°11'4" N 81°20'11" W The expedition crossed the Smoak Ranch en route from Fisheating Creek to Archbold Biological Station, where this bobcat, triggering a remote trail camera, stalks through the ancient scrub of Red Hill. Atop the Lake Wales Ridge south of Lake Placid, Archbold is a world-class research, education and conservation facility where the Florida Wildlife Corridor campaign was initiated during a bear workshop in December 2009.

27°11'17" N 81°21'8" W Zach Forsburg, working with the Orianne Society, uses radio telemetry to track the movements of eastern indigo snakes at Archbold Biological Station and surrounding ranches. The eastern indigo snake lives in upland sandhills throughout central Florida and the southeastern United States. Growing to nine feet, it is not only the longest native snake in North America, it also has the largest home range. Though road kill is the top form of indigo mortality, habitat loss and fragmentation are to blame for its federally threatened status. Declining gopher tortoise and eastern diamondback rattlesnake populations could also threaten indigo survival; indigos rely on tortoise burrows for nesting and rattlesnakes as a food source.

"On Monday we hiked from the Hendrie Ranch near Venus to Archbold Biological Station. Walking the station's fire lanes, especially during the dry season, is a chore. Tuesday was both a mental and physical workout, as we held a couple of workshops in the scrub with Archbold scientists, then after lunch we held a round table and interviewed with some media members."

– Joe Guthrie | Day 36

In the Everglades Headwaters, a mosaic of different agricultural uses can work together as a larger connected landscape. Examples in Highlands County include, clockwise from upper left: orange groves near Lake Istokpoga, palm hammock on the Roman III Ranch, bay forest on the Smoak Ranch and Fisheating Creek at Blue Head Ranch. Black bears, like this large male triggering a trail camera on the Hendrie Ranch, have shown researchers that male bears move widely in search of food, mates and denning sites.

27°4'52"N 81°19'11"W Black Bear

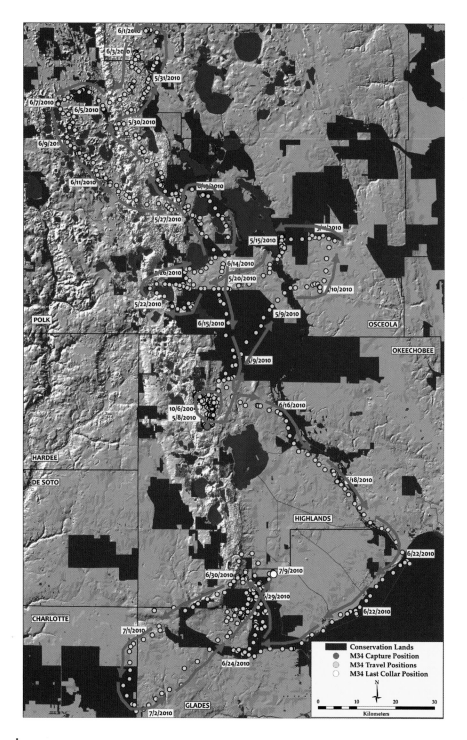

The following labels appear on the map:

6/1/2010
6/3/2010
5/31/2010
6/7/2010
6/5/2010
5/30/2010
6/9/2010
6/11/2010
5/27/2010
6/3/2010
5/15/2010
6/14/2010
6/20/2010
5/20/2010
6/10/2010
5/22/2010
5/9/2010
POLK
6/15/2010
OSCEOLA
OKEECHOBEE
3/9/2010
10/6/2009
5/8/2010
6/16/2010
HARDEE
DE SOTO
5/18/2010
HIGHLANDS
6/22/2010
6/30/2010
7/9/2010
5/29/2010
CHARLOTTE
7/1/2010
6/22/2010
6/24/2010
GLADES
7/2/2010

Conservation Lands
● M34 Capture Position
● M34 Travel Positions
○ M34 Last Collar Position

N

0   10   20   30
Kilometers

(essay continued from page vii) Dr. Harris mentored two other doctoral students whose work on wildlife movement and landscape conservation design inspired the Florida Wildlife Corridor campaign. Reed Noss and Tom Hoctor have both published visions of a statewide conservation network, dating back to Noss' work in the 1980s. Several decades of work on wildlife corridors enabled the Florida Wildlife Corridor campaign. Our route was based on a state corridor design called the Critical Linkages, which identify the best landscape connections between existing reserves. We used the blueprint of Tom's Critical Linkage database to define the area of the state we wanted to highlight via the expedition. Dr. Harris and Dr. Hoctor guided our initial steering committee, helping us name and outline the scope of the project. Our effort with the expedition campaign was built on a foundation of corridor and connectivity work that has been in the works in Florida for decades.

Dr. Harris devoted years thinking and writing about wildlife movement corridors, particularly their importance to wide ranging species in Florida, such as the black bear. To be a bear in south-central Florida is to be constantly moving in search of the most easily available food. Before they focus on the scrub, they are in the pine flatwoods eating saw palmetto berries, and before that they search out the best wild grapes and blackberries. After the scrub, they go to the oak hammocks to take advantage of the live oak acorn drop, which typically occurs later in the fall. A year is a cycle of shifting food resources for a bear, and the bears follow that cycle, changing habitat to track the fruiting of its favorite foods. Similar tracking occurs in males during the breeding season. Males travel widely in search of mates, and a dominant male may breed with 4-5 females. Finding that many females requires covering several hundred square miles. So while the land must provide the food hotspots and plentiful habitat, it also must allow for easy travel between the hotspots. These are some of the reasons we talk about corridors as important landscape features for wildlife conservation.

UK's research was intended to study movements and find patterns that might explain how the tiny bear population of the region keeps afloat in a landscape dominated by humans. Islands of forest – bayheads, flatwoods and palm-oak hammocks – are scattered throughout the region. The largest stands of forest exist on a handful of private ranches. Lowland forests buffer the streams, such as Fisheating Creek, which flows east into Lake Okeechobee. Between the forest patches is a mosaic of natural and semi-natural grasslands, much of which is utilized as pasture, cropland or citrus groves. A network of roads also laces through the landscape. Development is most intense along U.S. Highway 27, which runs along the sandy scrublands of the Lake Wales Ridge.

> *"These kinds of movements help us understand that these landscapes are still connected"* –Joe Guthrie | Day 36

The rest of Florida's black bear populations exist on large, contiguous blocks of public land, such as Ocala National Forest or in the Big Cypress region of south Florida. Like the Highlands/Glades bears, the seven different populations are mostly separate from one another due to past human persecution and habitat changes.

In order to understand the movement and behavior of our bears, we deployed GPS tracking collars on our animals. The collars were built with cell phone technology, so data from the animals arrived in our offices as SMS text messages every four hours. M34's collar data show that he stayed close to his capture site during the first eight months he wore it. He stayed mostly within the boundaries of the dense, dark bayhead forest between Sebring and the Avon Park Air Force Range.

On May 8, 2010, in the early stages of the breeding season, M34 made an abrupt exit from his traditional home range. He tracked northeast across the Air Force Range, bee-lining his way toward the Kissimmee River on the east boundary. With that first leap M34 began a journey that was fraught with danger for any bear, especially a hormone-charged and incautious young male. What ensued was a dispersal route that would amaze even those of us who'd been tracking bears for years. By the end of his two-month trek,

27°5'44" N 81°17'40" W Joe Guthrie fits a GPS tracking collar to M13, a 195-pound male black bear, on the Hendrie Ranch in Highlands County.

M34 would demonstrate astounding mobility and instinct for survival, all the while providing evidence of the landscape's fragile connectedness.

After crossing the Kissimmee River, M34 made for the south side of Lake Marion and the Adams Ranch. He lingered there for a week before turning back to the southwest, using Three Lakes Wildlife Management Area and then crossing the river again near the south end of the lake. He continued southwest until he came back to the Lake Wales Ridge and the town

of Frostproof in Polk County. He passed near the town in the night on May 22 and, finding nothing of interest, continued on his way, this time turning north and heading up the eastern edge of the Ridge. For the next eight days he traveled, staying in the forest except when crossing roads and open areas under cover of darkness. On May 26, he crossed busy SR 60, 10 miles east of Lake Wales, and headed north to Catfish Creek Preserve State Park. From Catfish Creek he continued north into the Upper Lakes Basin Watershed conservation area, finally arriving at the into the Upper Lakes Basin Watershed conservation area, finally arriving at the outskirts of Disney at Celebration on June 1. At I-4 he hung up, waiting out the day in a tiny patch of woods next to the Celebration Hospital, which sits at the intersection of the 417 toll road and I-4. Once darkness came he re-crossed 417 and headed south down I-4. For the next week he wandered southwest, at several points approaching the bustling interstate as if to cross.

At last, near the 46-mile marker (Polk City) on June 7, M34 turned back to the south. Again on a beeline he leapt south, crossing through Catfish Creek, Lake Kissimmee State Park, through the Bombing Range, passing his old home range near Sebring and continuing toward the Kissimmee River, where he entered the riparian corridor of the river on the June 16. From there he walked to the banks of Lake Okeechobee, swimming to the east bank and walking along the dike. For two days he walked the northwest shore of the great lake, before finding the mouth of Fisheating Creek in Glades County, on June 23. He spent a week back in the company of female bears, on a pair of private ranches that are the strongest population hubs for Highlands County bears. In all likelihood he found himself again outgunned by older males in this pristine, bear-populated haven.

As his collar was nearing its full data storage capacity, M34 made another dispersal trek from the Highlands/Glades population, circling west to the Babcock-Webb Wildlife Management Area of Charlotte County. Again finding little of interest, he turned back to the Fisheating Creek ranch complex after a week. On July 9, his collar reached maximum capacity and its automated release was triggered, enabling us to recover it from the field. His last known location was roughly 30 miles from where he began his dispersal, but still within the range of the Highlands/Glades population. In eight weeks, he had moved over 500 miles, spanning an area of roughly 110 miles north to south.

M34's route was a crucial piece of evidence when Carlton Ward Jr and Tom Hoctor were taking the first steps to unveil the Florida Wildlife Corridor vision and opportunity. It bore testament to the fact that the landscape held potential for dispersal by secretive wide-ranging wildlife and gave our project additional legitimacy. These findings were made possible by the determination of our colleagues at the University of Kentucky, former Maehr students John Cox and Wade Ulrey. John Cox stepped into the void left by Dave's tragic death and piloted the project forward as principal investigator. Wade returned to the project to be the field marshal in Florida.

Findings from the M34 data and the rest of the bears we collared suggested that the Highlands/Glades black bear represents an ecological microcosm of the entire Florida peninsula. It has a solid toehold in several key areas, just like our large public conservation lands. In order to survive, the black bear must be able to move between its strongholds. Overlapping needs for black bear movement, Florida panther survival, plentiful clean water for the Everglades and Florida's ranching and outdoor heritage were all compelling angles on the same story. Florida must maintain its ecological connectedness.

The vision of a connected natural Florida is not new. We put a new name on the idea, and using social media and compelling art, we tried to tell a story that Florida and the world needs to know. The background – M34, Dave, Dr. Harris, Tom Hoctor's science – was never far from my mind as we traipsed our way north on the expedition. We were allowed an almost uninterrupted view of the world as M34 might have seen it. We were following in his footsteps, and those of untold numbers of other bears, panthers, Native Americans, cracker cow hunters and explorers. We were also following the lead of many who have worked to ensure that the opportunity still exists.

27°11′4″N 81°20′11″W The matrix of public and private lands along the Lake Wales Ridge in Highlands County supports a diversity of wildlife, captured here by camera-traps around Archbold Biological Station. Clockwise from top left: Florida panther, raccoon, white-tailed deer and coyote.

27°28'28" N 81°33'8" W A diverse assemblage of trees, including old-growth cypress, cabbage palms, oaks and pines, fill the lush forests of Highlands Hammock State Park. One live oak is 1,000 years old and measures 36 feet around the trunk. Situated along the Lake Wales Ridge near Sebring and the Kissimmee River to the east, Highlands Hammock provides a habitat for wildlife, including the Florida black bear.

"If you can work with ranchers and other landowners to help store water on their properties by having it flooded in a natural, historic way during certain times of the year, that accomplishes many of the water cleaning objectives and more. It helps restore the wetlands, improve the wildlife habitat and clean the water in natural ways."

– Carlton Ward Jr | Day 45

27°22'47" N 81°22'59" W   Joe Guthrie navigates Josephine Creek. The narrow creek corridor connects scrub habitats and a chain of lakes along the Lake Wales Ridge with Lake Istokpoga and is one the few natural connections remaining in Highlands County where wildlife can cross U.S. Highway 27.

27°33'7" N 81°21'26" W From Lake Istokpoga, the expedition paddled north to the inflow of Arbuckle Creek and then upstream for 20 miles to Rafter T Ranch, which the dark creek separates from Avon Park Air Force Range, delineated by cypress trees in the background. The pond in the foreground is an example of collaboration between private ranches and the South Florida Water Management District to help restore the Everglades by storing and naturally filtering water in historic wetlands throughout the headwaters.

27°32'38" N 81°15'59" W An open canopy of longleaf pines provides intermittent shade to an understory of cutthroat grass, a rare endemic species found only in central Florida. The scene is from Avon Park Air Force Range, which provides an excellent example of how military readiness and natural resource conservation can work together. The 106,000-acre base between Arbuckle Creek and the Kissimmee River protects the largest remaining extent of cutthroat grass in the world along with a variety of endangered plants and animals. The expedition met a special operations unit there practicing to intercept hostile boats on the open seas. One commando shares how his colleague recently used a 50-caliber rifle to shoot out the engine blocks of a cigarette boat trying to outrun their Blackhawk helicopter between the Bahamas and Miami.

"Hot brass rains down around us from the Blackhawk helicopter hovering overhead, as cartridge casings pepper the palmettos and pine limbs swaying in the downdraft. Muzzle blasts crack through the hum of the rotors, followed by staccato pings of full metal jacket rounds smacking steel silhouettes standing in the distance." – Carlton Ward Jr | Day 43

27°33'20" N 81°11'15" W Dry bag in hand, Elam Stoltzfus swims across the Kissimmee River between Avon Park Air Force Range and Kissimmee Prairie Preserve State Park. Just upstream, an aerial view shows the river winding between the two properties. A few years before, the river here was a wide, straight channel that had been dredged in the 1960s. By restoring natural curves, hydrologists have successfully slowed the flow, rehydrated historic wetlands, enhanced wildlife habitat and helped clean the water moving south toward Lake Okeechobee and the Everglades.

27°34'50" N 81°1'44" W Jen Benson and biologist Paul Gray listen for the faint call of the Florida grasshopper sparrow, arguably the most endangered bird in North America. Kissimmee Prairie Preserve State Park protects the largest expanse of native dry prairie in Florida, hosting sparrows and numerous other species of wildlife. Aside from scattered palmettos, the sweeping prairie views are reminiscent of the Great Plains. Bison may have roamed here as recently as the 1700s. The Kissimmee Prairie is a core landscape in the Florida Wildlife Corridor and several cattle ranches in the region are high priorities for inclusion in the new Everglades Headwaters National Wildlife Refuge and Conservation Area.

27°39'14" N 80°57'23" W The Kissimmee Prairie ecosystem extends north of Kissimmee Prairie Preserve State Park toward the Kissimmee Chain of Lakes. The property in this photograph near Yeehaw Junction was recently slated for a new city called Destiny that aspires to build 100,000 homes here in the Everglades Headwaters. Construction has not yet begun and state federal agencies have also targeted this land for protection via acquisition or a conservation easement.

27°54'3" N 81°18'55" W Clint Lightsey and his daughter Hattie drive an Angus cow and calf across their family ranch beside Lake Kissimmee. The Lightsey family has been ranching in Florida since the 1850s and Hattie represents the 15th generation of her family ranching in America. Because the Lightseys have protected their property with perpetual conservation easements, Hattie is ensured the opportunity to continue the legacy and the people of Florida are guaranteed that this important piece of the Everglades Headwaters will remain natural.

"To realize that these ranchers believe enough in what we are doing to give that much of their time and come share it with us is really humbling, one of the things I'll never forget."

– Carlton Ward Jr | Day 52

28°3'23" N 81°24'59" W Cattle ranchers and conservationists from the Northern Everglades Alliance host the expedition for a 17-mile trail ride that begins at the Creek Ranch on Lake Hatchineha, traverses South Florida Water Management District conservation land and arrives at The Nature Conservancy's Disney Wilderness Preserve. The Creek Ranch is adjacent to the first piece of the new Everglades Headwaters National Wildlife Refuge and Conservation Area, commemorated in a belt buckle based on a photograph by Carlton Ward Jr. Refuge manager Charlie Pelizza presented the buckle to the expedition team during the trek. One of the primary purposes of the new refuge is to protect the working ranches of the Everglades Headwaters.

"Most people live on Florida's coast and don't know that this incredible corridor down the middle of the state even exists."

– Mallory Lykes Dimmitt | Day 50

28°6′12″ N 81°25′31″ W The red-cockaded woodpecker is an endangered species surviving in pockets of longleaf pine forest throughout the Everglades Headwaters and Florida Wildlife Corridor. Biologist Jennifer Millikowsky studies an individual at The Nature Conservancy's Disney Wilderness Preserve, where researchers have successfully reintroduced the bird and established nine different colonies. Indicating a functionally connected landscape, one individual bird recently colonized the Disney Wilderness Preserve by flying 40 miles from its original home at Avon Park Air Force Range.

28°3'24" N 81°9'11" W Ranches throughout the Everglades Headwaters support abundant bird life. A burowing owl, left, feeds on a mole cricket at Camp Lonesome Ranch in Osceola County. Clockwise from top left: meadowlark, Buck Island Ranch; sandhill cranes, Lightsey Ranch at Tiger Lake; Osceola turkeys, Lake X Ranch; and crested caracara, Blue Head Ranch.

28°7′37″ N 81°25′9″ W Large cypress trees stand along the edge of Lake Russell at The Nature Conservancy's Disney Wilderness Preserve. Near suburban Kissimmee, this is one of the last undeveloped lakes in central Florida. It connects to Reedy Creek, the Kissimmee Chain of Lakes, the Kissimmee River and Lake Okeechobee. Projects working to restore the flow of water south from Lake Okeechobee into the Shark River Slough will allow rainfall filling Lake Russell to trace a more natural course through the peninsula toward Florida Bay. Reconnecting the watershed will also help connect the landscape for wildlife.

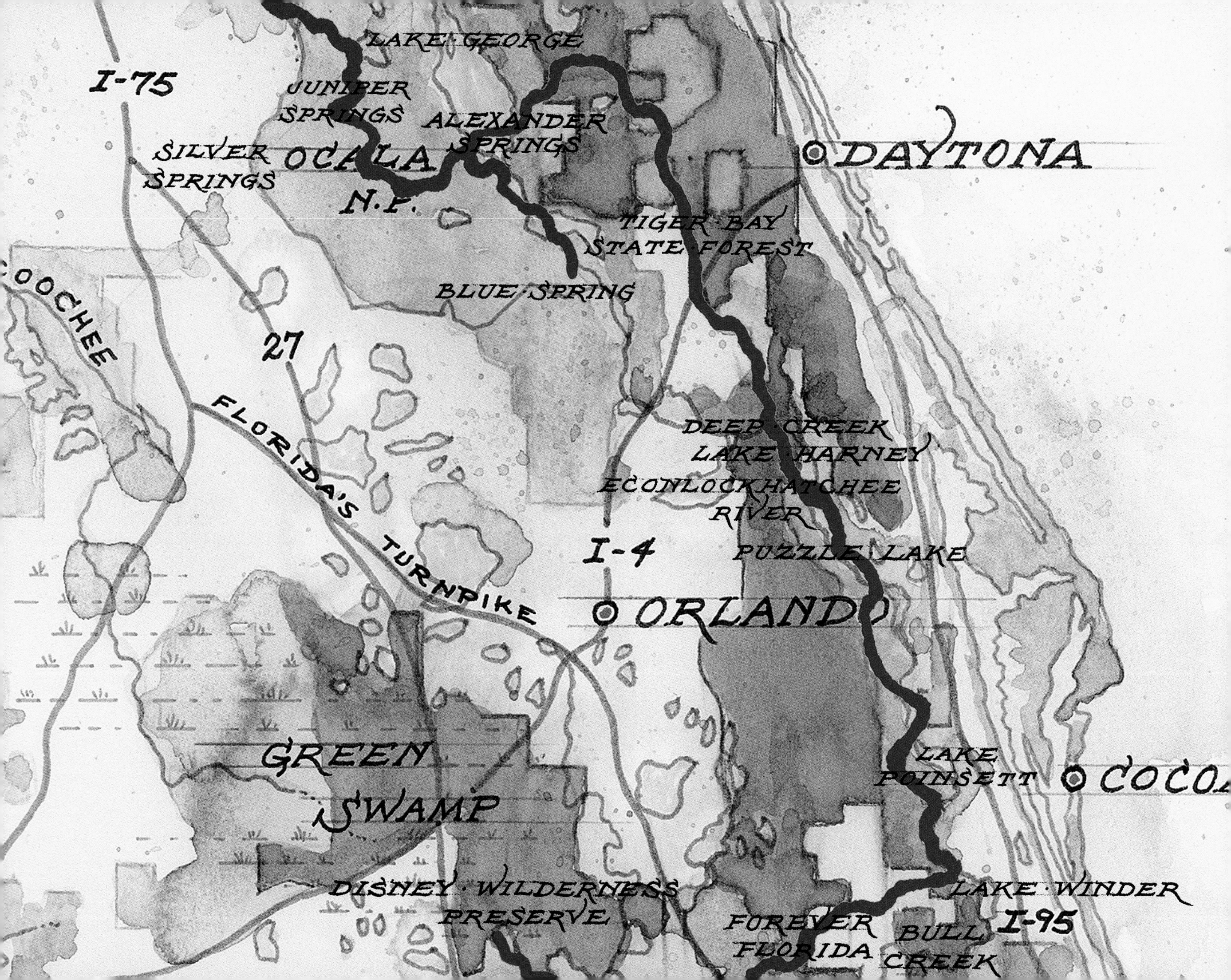

I-75

LAKE·GEORGE

JUNIPER
SPRINGS
ALEXANDER
SPRINGS

SILVER   OCALA
SPRINGS   N.F.

27

FLORIDA'S·TURNPIKE

COOCHEE

GREEN

SWAMP

DISNEY·WILDERNESS
PRESERVE

ODAYTONA

TIGER·BAY
STATE·FOREST

BLUE·SPRING

DEEP·CREEK
LAKE·HARNEY
ECONLOCKHATCHEE
RIVER

I-4   PUZZLE·LAKE

O ORLANDO

LAKE
POINSETT   O COCO

LAKE·WINDER
I-95
FOREVER   BULL
FLORIDA   CREEK

ST. JOHNS RIVER

Hiking through Three Lakes Wildlife Management Area, the expedition transitions from the Everglades Headwaters to the headwaters of the St. Johns River. After trekking through Bull Creek Wildlife Management Area and visiting Deseret Ranch, the team begins a weeklong paddle downstream from Lake Winder through Lake Poinsett, by Tosohatchee Wildlife Management Area, St. Johns National Wildlife Refuge and Seminole Ranch Conservation Area, through Puzzle Lake, around the Econlockhatchee River delta and up Deep Creek. From there they continue overland through the Volusia Conservation Corridor across Farmton, Palm Bluff Conservation Area, Lefils Ranch, Longleaf Pine Preserve, Interstate 4, Tiger Bay State Forest, Plum Creek Timberlands, Heart Island Conservation Area and Lake George State Forest.

28°23'23" N 80°52'58" W The 310-mile-long St. Johns River is the longest in Florida and drops only 30 feet in elevation, or about one inch per mile, over its length. It originates from flat marshlands south of Vero Beach, swells into numerous lakes, such as Puzzle Lake, above, and enters the Atlantic in Jacksonville. It is one of a few rivers in the country that flow from south to north. Nearly four million people live within its watershed.

27°59'21" N 81°1'59" W The 1400-mile Florida Trail is one of 11 National Scenic Trails in the United States. The expedition enjoys a beautiful section through Three Lakes Wildlife Management Area in Osceola County, where they cross Florida's version of a continental divide, walking out of the Everglades Headwaters and into the headwaters of the St. Johns River. From Three Lakes, the Florida Trail leads northeast into Bull Creek Wildlife Management Area, protecting Crabgrass Creek and Bull Creek as they flow north into the St. Johns River. In addition to hiking and camping, the Bull Creek property provides opportunities for horseback riding and seasonal hunting.

28°6'23" N 80°55'51" W Crabgrass Creek

"We still have a chance to connect these core natural areas throughout our state. There's a huge amount of opportunity. That opportunity exits in the land, and that opportunity exists even more importantly in the people who are the stewards of that land."

– Carlton Ward Jr | Day 54

28°11'10" N 80°52'35" W   Further north, near Holopaw, cowboy Travis Brown parts a herd of heifers in cowpens at Deseret Ranch, which encompasses nearly 300,000 acres between Orlando and Cocoa. Deseret Ranch is the top producer of beef cattle in North America and is joined by five other Florida ranches ranked in the top 10 in the country.

28°2'45" N 81°0'1" W   Along the Florida National Scenic Trail between Kenansville and St. Cloud, Forever Florida offers eco-safaris, with activities ranging from canopy tours to overnight horseback adventures, where visitors can experience the wildlife and cultural heritage of a Florida cattle ranch. Forever Florida manages herds of cracker cattle and cracker horses descended from the first cattle and horses to arrive in America, from Spain to Florida in 1521.

28°26′44″ N 80°53′24″ W Joe Guthrie launches over the St. Johns from a rope swing near Tosohatchee Wildlife Management Area. Tosohatchee protects 19 miles of river frontage in eastern Orange County and buffers the headwaters from Orlando.

28°21'46" N 80°52'29" W The expedition enters the St. Johns River in Lake Winder and begins a weeklong paddle downstream through the relatively well-protected headwaters. Just north of Lake Poinsett, the Mulberry Indian Mound rises more than 20 feet above the surrounding floodplain.

"We've been on the move, and sometimes it takes all the energy that I have just to get from point A to point B. Some of my best moments are early in the morning, and especially when we're on the waterways and the fog comes in. And I crawl out of the tent, get into the kayak, mount the camera, and then I'm at work. It's right there."

– Elam Stoltzfus | Day 62

29°11'40" N 81°34'34" W St. John's River

28°29'45" N 80°52'57" W On day 62 of the expedition, Elam Stoltzfus films from his kayak in the St. Johns River as the sun rises over Canaveral Marshes Conservation Area. Further downstream, the river traces a silver path through Ocala National Forest, just before flowing into Lake George. The St. Johns River is the second largest watershed in the state. The margins of its headwaters are relatively well protected by a network of state and federal conservation properties.

28°41'42" N 81°2'4" W   An island of sabal palms catches the late afternoon sun near the Econlockhatchee River's confluence with the St. Johns River, just north of Puzzle Lake. The 55-mile-long Econlockhatchee and its 150 miles of creeks is a primary tributary to the St. Johns.

28°43′58″ N 81°2′44″ W A flock of white pelicans takes flight from a sandbar near the southern inlet to Lake Harney. Thousands of birds migrate to this region of the St. Johns each year, in part following shad—a species of fish that makes a 150-mile annual migration from the Atlantic Ocean near Jacksonville to these stretches of the Upper St. Johns. Public lands, such as Little Big Econ State Forest, pictured left along the Econlockhatchee River, help maintain the health of the watershed and associated wildlife.

28°41′37″ N 81°2′21″ W Econlockhatchee River

28°18′13″ N 80°48′14″ W A cottonmouth, the only venomous water snake in the United States, swims with ease across the St. Johns River.

28°47′44″ N 81°3′28″ W A limpkin forages for freshwater mussels in the shallow margins where Deep Creek meets the St. Johns.

"Conservationists and landowners really have a lot of common goals. When you're a sixth, seventh or eighth-generation Florida rancher or farmer, you want your children and grandchildren to have the opportunity to continue that heritage. Without the land, that's not possible." – Carlton Ward Jr | Day 67

28°54'51" N 81°8'27" W Jim Lefils is a cattle rancher and forester who recently worked with his family, Volusia County and the St. Johns River Water Management District to protect their lands through a conservation easement. The collaboration completes a key link in the Volusia Conservation Corridor, a county initiative within the larger Florida Wildlife Corridor, making it possible for the expedition to be the first people to travel its full length.

I-95

TIMBERLANDS

CAMP·BLANDING

ST·JOHNS

ETONIAH·CREEK
STATE·FOREST

TIMBERLANDS

RICE·CREEK
CONSERVATION·AREA

OCKLAWAHA
RIVER

FLORIDA·TRAIL

LAKE·GEORGE

I-75

JUNIPER
SPRINGS   ALEXANDER
SPRINGS

SILVER   OCALA
SPRINGS   N.F.

⊙ DAYTONA

TIGER·BAY
STATE·FOREST

BLUE·SPRING

LACOOCHEE

27

LE⊙

OCALA FOREST & SPRINGS

From Lake George State Forest, the expedition crosses the St. Johns River to enter Ocala National Forest. After paddling to explore Blue Spring State Park, the team hikes the Florida National Scenic Trail from Alexander Springs to the Ocklawaha River with additional camps at Juniper Springs, Hopkins Prairie and Lake Delancy. The trek continues into the Ocala to Osceola Corridor, visiting Rice Creek Conservation Area, Etoniah Creek State Forest and Belmore State Forest, moving toward the Camp Blanding Joint Training Center.

29°7'38" N 81°39'24" W A clearing in Ocala National Forest near Farles Prairie provides seasonal wetlands and habitat for wildlife, including a mother bear and two cubs that were spotted along the edge of the timber during a flyover.

"I just want to share how amazing this middle part of the state is, down the whole spine, and how much of an opportunity there is to protect it. The time is right to do so, now."

– Mallory Lykes Dimmitt | Day 78

29°25'34" N 81°47'25" W At the Lake Delancy campground, Mallory Dimmitt prepares for a day of hiking on the Florida National Scenic Trail through the 383,000-acre Ocala National Forest. The trail will traverse some of the state's best longleaf pine habitat, its open quality maintained by prescribed fires.

29°26'44" N 81°48'14" W Longleaf pines

"I kick hard against the current which speeds across shallow limestone and sand, making slow progress toward the headspring. The mullet and garfish pointed in the same direction seem to move so effortlessly. I push to keep up with Margaret Ross Tolbert, renowned painter and siren of Florida's springs."

- Carlton Ward Jr | Day 73

28°56'51" N 81°20'23" W Blue Spring State Park in Volusia County protects the largest spring on the St. Johns River. A fallen tree lies across the main vent, silhouetted against the sun and surrounding trees. The average flow is 165 million gallons per day. The relatively warm 72 degree water makes Blue Spring an important winter refuge for manatees living in the St. Johns River. Renowned painter Margaret Ross Tolbert hosts the expedition there for an exploration of the watery world she depicts and strives to protect with her art.

29°4'53" N 81°34'41" W Another of Florida's 27 first magnitude springs, Alexander Springs also flows into the St. Johns River. It is easily accessible along the Florida National Scenic Trail in Ocala National Forest. Joe Guthrie free dives into one of the sandy vents where courting river cooters swim through the eelgrass.

29°27'1" N 81°51'20" W When botanical explorer William Bartram came to Florida in the 1700s, he described a landscape where he could see for miles beneath canopies of grandiose pines. Longleaf pine forests, pictured here with an understory of wiregrass in Ocala National Forest, once covered 90 million acres across the southeast. Logging and development have cut them to just three percent of their historic range. Patches of forest that remain provide essential stepping stones for the Florida Wildlife Corridor.

29°15'56" N 81°41'10" W Joe Guthrie, lead, and Elam Stoltzfus hike beneath arching oak limbs beside a palmetto-lined ridge on the Florida National Scenic Trail as the expedition approaches Hopkins Prairie in Ocala National Forest.

29°12'49" N 82°2'23" W The Silver River slices through the east side of Ocala National Forest, carrying crystal clear water to the Ocklawaha and St. Johns Rivers. Silver Springs, famous for glass-bottom boat rides, supplies the river more than 550 million gallons per day, making it the largest spring in Florida. The flow is steadily declining as urban and agricultural consumption drains the aquifer. Controversial proposals for greater pumping further threaten this Florida icon.

"When you walk eight hours a day and feel the grass, you feel the water, you feel the mud, you feel the rain come down on you, you're so in touch. You're so in tune with nature. Your sleeping habits change. You go to bed when it's dark, and you wake up when the sun comes up. It's like you get that rhythm of nature. So I hope I never lose that."

– Elam Stoltzfus | Day 79

29°13'53" N 82°0'20" W Private forestry operations cover many millions of acres in northern Florida. Managed forests provide excellent wildlife habitat and can serve as essential landscape linkages in the Florida Wildlife Corridor. This mixed hardwood and pine forest adjacent to Ocala National Forest near Silver Springs, owned by Rayonier, is an example of the company's commitment to conservation and sustainable forestry. Rayonier is the fourth largest private landowner in Florida with over 420,000 acres.

29°26'9" N 81°48'31" W A Sherman's fox squirrel, the largest species of tree squirrel, pauses among the branches of an oak in Ocala National Forest. Oak hammocks and pine forests provide important habitat for fox squirrels and other wildlife that prefer relatively open understories, such as the sweeping wiregrass, right, maintained by frequent fire. The natural diversity of a healthy longleaf pine forest is comparable to that of tropical rain forests, with more than 40 species per square meter.

29°28'28" N 81°51'27" W Longleaf Pine Forest

"And I think that because of the people and the contacts and the relationships that came out of this, that's what makes it last forever. It's not about the video, it's not about the film, but it's about connecting people. To me, that's what this is about."

— Elam Stoltzfus | Day 81

29°48'28" N 81°51'7" W Bruce Hill, Florida Forest Service District Manger, reviews a map of Belmore State Forest with Joe Guthrie, center, and Elam Stoltzfus. The expedition explored a series of state forests while navigating the Ocala to Osceola Corridor, including Etoniah Creek State Forest, which protects a species of plant—Etoniah Rosemary—occuring nowhere else in the world.

29°45'11" N 81°50'7" W Etoniah Rosemary

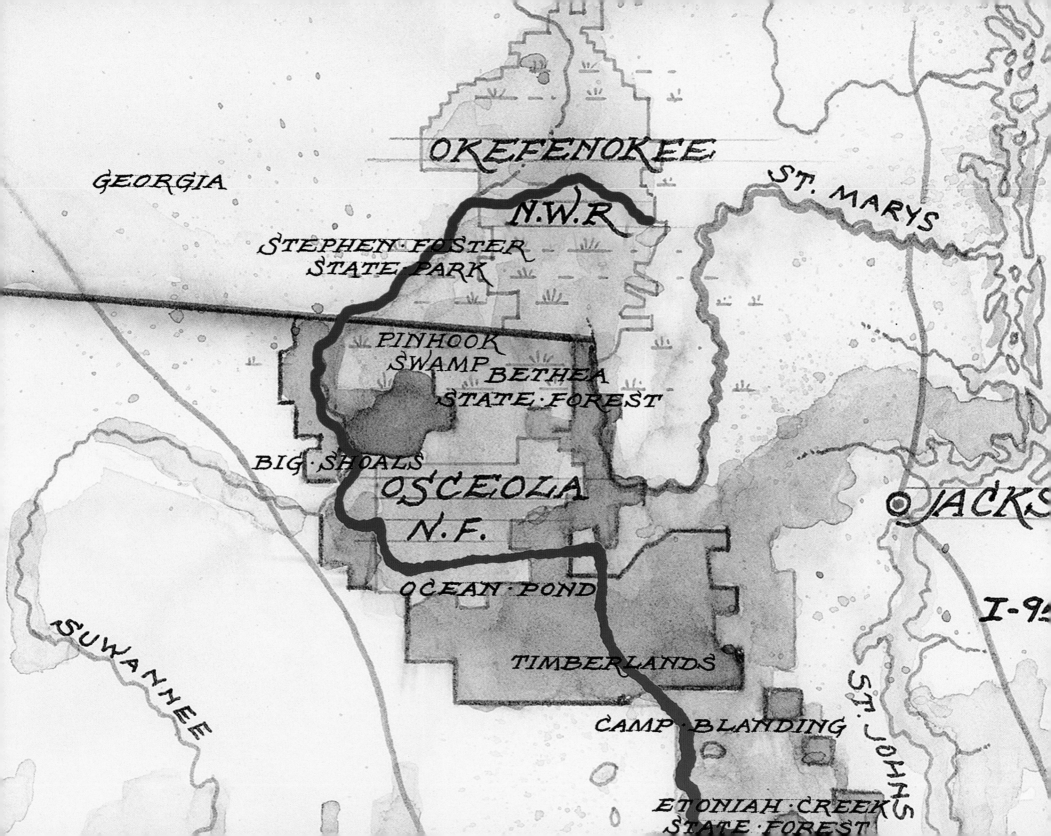

OSCEOLA, SUWANNEE & OKEFENOKEE

In the northern reaches of the Ocala to Osceola Corridor, the expedition crosses Camp Blanding, Lake Butler Wildlife Management Area, and a variety of private timber plantations before arriving at Olustee Battlefield Historic State Park and Osceola National Forest. Learning of a 30,000-acre wildfire burning in the Pinhook Swamp near their planned route to the Georgia border, the team veers west on the Florida Trail through Osceola National Forest to enter the Suwannee River just upstream from Big Shoals. They then paddle upstream on the Suwannee for five days before crossing the Georgia border and exploring the river's headwaters in the swamps of Okefenokee National Wildlife Refuge.

30°35'42" N 82°41'51" W The expedition team, from front to back: Carlton Ward Jr, Mallory Dimmitt, Elam Stoltzfus and Joe Guthrie paddle the Suwannee River upstream on day 95, less than a mile south of the Georgia-Florida line (photo by Genevieve Dimmitt).

"*Camp Blanding is a major hub in the corridor that the State is trying to understand—especially when it comes to the black bear.*" *– Joe Guthrie | Day 84*

30°2'2" N 81°59'3" W Camp Blanding is a 73,000-acre Army and Air National Guard training facility in Clay County that includes a 56,000-acre Wildlife Management Area that the public can enjoy. Natural habitats include hardwood hammocks along the headwaters of Jack Creek and longleaf pine forests such as these, which support a population of red-cockaded woodpeckers. Bear research here is revealing the corridor connections between Ocala National Forest to the south and Osceola National Forest to the north.

"I would say the most unpleasant surprise is when you make a corner on your bike and you come around to the next road, and it's white, deep sugar sand. That is a really sinking feeling because, literally, your back tire will sink in and you won't be able to ride through it. So, in the last week we spent a lot of time walking our bikes."

— *Mallory Lykes Dimmitt | Day 87*

"Chiggers, ticks, smilax and blackberry thorns, scratch marks, poison ivy, mosquitoes, blisters."

— *Mallory Lykes Dimmitt | Day 88*

30°5'8" N 82°17'36" W Mallory Dimmitt powers through sugar sand during a 33-mile bicycle crossing of Lake Butler Wildlife Management Area and surrounding timberlands en route from Camp Blanding to Osceola National Forest. This 200,000-acre forest, seen at right from a fire tower, is a mosaic of low pine ridges separated by cypress and bay swamps. The vast Pinhook Swamp is a regional wildlife corridor success; protecting it saved natural connections across the Florida-Georgia line, between Osceola National Forest and the Okefenokee National Wildlife Refuge.

30°19'23" N 82°33'32" W Osceola National Forest

30°48'20" N 82°24'48" W In the upper reaches of the Suwannee River, Carlton Ward Jr, left, and Joe Guthrie paddle beneath bright spring foliage (photo by Mac Stone). Further downstream an Ogeechee Tupelo spreads its branches over a shallow sandbar colored orange by the tannin-stained water flowing from the Okefenokee Swamp. The Suwannee River runs 240 miles from the Okefenokee National Wildlife Refuge in southern Georgia through the Lower Suwannee National Wildlife Refuge to the Gulf of Mexico near Cedar Key.

"The trees here are bizarre and beautiful at once. The tupelos and pond cypress seem to compete for which can place the most attention grabbing form along these sandy bluffs. The tupelo trunks twist and bulge and fold over themselves in bizarre, buddha-like shapes. Their roots spill out from the trunk and fall toward the inky blackwater in disorganized cascades. The cypress are anchored to the bank by massive, furrowed and bulbous bases, suddenly tapering to a small bole, usually less than 50 feet tall."

– Joe Guthrie | Day 96

30°33'45" N 82°43'23" W Ogeechee Tupelo tree

30°48'7" N 82°13'10" W Flowers bloom throughout the freshwater prairies of the Okefenokee Swamp. The rich blue of the savanna iris and distinct shape of the grass pink orchid stand out against the marsh grasses, while a fragrant water lily opens its pedals toward the twilight sky. The Okefenokee National Wildlife Refuge protects 402,000 acres of wilderness, including one of America's oldest and best preserved freshwater systems at the headwaters to the Suwannee and St. Marys Rivers.

30°48'23" N 82°14'28" W Water lily

30°47'57" N 82°25'23" W Entering the Okefenokee National Wildlife Refuge, the rain begins to subside and a prothonotary warbler forages among the low branches of a tupelo tree. Northern Florida and southern Georgia provide summer home ranges to these birds that migrate to the tropics during winter. Prothonotary warblers nest in tree cavities—uncommon behavior that may be an adaptation to living in flooded forests.

30°33'37" N 82°43'23" W During the expedition's last few miles in Florida, Mallory Dimmitt leads paddling through spring rain. Rainfall gathering here and in the Okefenokee Swamp a few miles upstream flows 240 miles to Gulf of Mexico, where clean freshwater is essential to the health of the Suwannee estuary and its commercial fisheries.

"A night in the swamp after a heavy rain, all the frogs, the chirping, the owls, it's like a symphony. But to me that's silence compared to the roar and high decibel noises of the city."

— Elam Stoltzfus | Day 97

30°46'13" N 82°28'23" W Carlton Ward Jr paddles into the sunrise near the headwaters of the Suwannee River in southern Georgia. The solar panel in the back of the kayak is used to charge camera batteries and power communications equipment (photo by Mac Stone). Glistening in the rain, a young alligator smiles for the camera in the Okefenokee Swamp. Okefenokee is translated from Indian words meaning "land of the trembling earth." The peat deposits, up to 15 feet thick, are so unstable in spots that stomping the surface can cause surrounding trees and bushes to tremble.

30°48'19" N 82°25'7" W Alligator

30°49'24" N 82°23'0" W During the first night camping in the Okefenokee, Joe Guthrie lights a fire in the rain and people gather to glean wisdom from National Geographic Explorer-in-Residence, Michael Fay, center, who joined the expedition for the final days, standing with photographer Mac Stone, right, and videographer Joe Davenport.

30°48'13" N 82°13'12" W Starlight illuminates the swamp on the final night in the Okefenokee. There is a nice symmetry to completing the expedition in this great Georgia wilderness, in many ways similar to the Everglades where the journey began 100 days before. The entire Florida peninsula lies in between, along with a remarkable opportunity to keep the Everglades and Okefenokee connected.

30°49'26" N 82°22'57" W From front to back, Michael Fay, Elam Stoltzfus, Joe Guthrie, Mallory Dimmitt and Carlton Ward Jr walk from the Mixon's Hammock campsite to their boats. They will paddle to Georgia's Stephen C. Foster State Park for an Earth Day event celebrating the Florida Wildlife Corridor opportunity (photo by Mac Stone).

"I'd like to have everybody in Florida come walk with us, and to see these things firsthand. I can assure you that if they did, they would be behind this idea. Short of that, I hope that through the film, photography and writing we at least capture their imaginations about this opportunity so together we can get it done. "

– Carlton Ward Jr | Day 98

"What I'm realizing, the more I learn, I have an entire lifetime of stories right here within 200 miles of my home that really need a voice. And I hope that I can continue to work in this vein and we can help find ways for others to really engage and speak up for these special places in Florida that everyone needs to know about. In terms of cultural differences, you can get on a plane to Timbuktu, Mali to experience something else. Or you can get in a car or a boat and go 20 miles in Florida and discover another world. The coastal world of new Florida needs to know about this other world. Because without it, we don't have food, we don't have water, we don't have wildlife. If people know about it, they'll appreciate it and they'll love it the way we do. That's the first step to helping protect it."

– Carlton Ward Jr | Day 99

28°5'28" N 81°24'19" W Longleaf pines cast long shadows in the morning fog, backlit by the first rays of day. The Nature Conservancy's Disney Wilderness Preserve, in the Everglades Headwaters, serves as a gateway from suburban Kissimmee and Orlando into the Florida Wildlife Corridor.

PHOTOGRAPHY NOTES

30°46'14" N 82°28'27" W Carlton photographs the upper Suwannee River on day 96 of the expedition (photo by Mac Stone).

All of the photographs in this book come from places within the Florida Wildlife Corridor. Most were shot from the trail during the 100-day expedition. Others are from prior assignments or reconnaissance flights. All of the photographs were captured with a documentary photojournalism approach—the images represent natural scenes or moments in front of the lens; content is never added or removed and there have been no computer alterations or enhancements beyond modest adjustments for cropping, color and contrast (the same tools used in film darkrooms). The panoramic photographs running across two pages are high-resolution composites of several individual photographs stitched together in Photoshop.

The photographs of the bobcat on page 51, black bear on page 55 and wildlife on page 59 were captured with custom-made camera traps, each consisting of a Trailmaster 1500 infrared beam that triggers a

Nikon camera and three Nikon strobes, combined with specialized weather casings, wiring harnesses, brackets and camouflaging. These systems were based on designs I developed for photographing leopards in Gabon and desert elephants in Mali. By adding external battery systems and solar arrays, the Florida versions were capable of providing a full year of continual trail monitoring. Each was toppled by a bear at least once. One bear stole a flash and never returned it. Additional camera trap photographs can be seen on my website.

I shot 29,263 photographs during the expedition, mostly with lightweight Nikon dSLRs. While hiking, I carried one camera body, a wide-angle zoom, a telephoto zoom and a 1:1 macro lens. When working from a boat, I added a second camera body and 400 mm telephoto to the kit. All photographs were geo-tagged by either on-camera gps or syncing gps tracks with digital timestamps. Photography was a primary tool of the mainstream and social media outreach during the trek. Images were captioned in the field and selections were uploaded via computer or directly from smartphones whenever we had signal. Camera, phone and computer batteries were charged from solar panels or rechargeable battery packs. I only killed one lens during the trek, dunking it and the attached camera in Josephine Creek. I resurrected the camera by baking it in a convection oven while visiting Rafter T Ranch and it somehow kept working for the next 60 days. iPhones were also very useful for documenting the journey, especially for social media posts. LifeProof provided cases that protected the phones well enough to use them for underwater photography.

About the Photographer

Carlton Ward Jr is a conservation photographer from Tampa, Florida. His passion for nature was born from the Florida landscape, where eight generations of family history have shaped his perspective. Through his photographs, he aims to promote the conservation of natural environments and cultural legacies.

Carlton is a founding fellow of the International League of Conservation Photographers (ILCP) and president of the Legacy Institute for Nature & Culture (LINC), a non-profit organization with the purpose of celebrating and protecting Florida's natural and cultural heritage through art. He completed a Master's degree in Ecology while working for the Smithsonian Institution in Gabon, leading to his first book, *The Edge of Africa*. He has since worked with the WILD Foundation to photograph an endangered herd of migratory desert elephants in Mali. He is currently focused on long-term conservation projects at home and is a grantee of the National Geographic Society for leading the Florida Wildlife Corridor Expedition.

Carlton's photographs are widely exhibited and featured in magazines including *Audubon*, *Geo*, *Smithsonian*, *Nature Conservancy* and *National Wildlife*. His 2009 Book, *Florida Cowboys*, won a silver medal in the Florida Book Awards and *Popular Photography Magazine* featured him as one of three photographers working to save vanishing America.

Limited-edition prints of select photographs are available through CarltonWard.com where you can also connect to his blog and social media channels.

ACKNOWLEDGMENTS

We would like to thank the members of the original steering committee who in early 2010 helped shape the Florida Wildlife Corridor vision. Participants included: John Cox, Eric Draper, Manley Fuller, Joe Guthrie, Larry Harris, Richard Hilsenbeck, Tom Hoctor, Charles Lee, Sarah Lynch, Tricia Martin, Julie Morris, Laurie McDonald, Reed Noss, Mary Oakley, Charles Pattison, Preston Robertson, Brian Scheick, Dave Shindle, Dan Smith, Hilary Swain, Carlton Ward Jr, George Willson, Jim Wood and Wade Ulrey.

We would also like to thank academic pioneers of wildlife corridor thinking in Florida who helped lay the foundation for this project, including: Larry Harris, Tom Hoctor, David Maehr and Reed Noss.

Tom Hoctor, Richard Hilsenbeck and Carlton Ward Jr designed the Florida Wildlife Corridor map, an original watercolor painting by Mike Reagan, based on corridor priorities from the Conservation Trust for Florida and the Florida Ecological Greenways Network.

There are many organizations that work hard to protect natural Florida and places within the Florida Wildlife Corridor. We encourage you to visit FloridaWildlifeCorridor.org to view the full list of partners and support them.

The leading sponsors of the Florida Wildlife Corridor Expedition were the National Geographic Society, the Everglades Foundation and Nell Ward. Please visit our website for a more complete list of expedition sponsors. The Florida Wildlife Corridor film and exhibit were funded by Mosaic.

We thank Salter-Mitchell for donating website design and for their professional communications services during the expedition. We also thank WUSF for producing weekly reports for Florida and National Public Radio, as well as all of the mainstream media outlets that helped share our story.

There are four unsung members of expedition team whose work behind the scenes made everything possible. Tom Hoctor helped with much of the route planning, including a few changes on the fly, and organized several great outreach events along the way. Rick Smith deserves special recognition for location coordination and logistical support of every variety throughout the entire trek, from driving the trailer to facilitating re-supplies, even doing laundry and cooking. Lisa Baylor gracefully transitioned from photography studio manager to running base camp during the expedition and for a full year prior and following. Videographer Joe Davenport was with us throughout the journey, camera rolling. His production skills made the weekly TV segments possible and his company invariably improved camp morale.

During the expedition, we crossed a different public or private property nearly every day. Listing all of the landowners, agencies and people who helped us along the way would require several pages. To everyone who lent a hand, joined us on the trail or helped share the story, please accept our sincere gratitude. We could have not done it without you.

We also thank our families for moral support and allowing 100 days on the trail. The Dimmitts, Wards, Stoltzfuses and Guthries all joined us at different stages. Friends from the Swann and Lazanis families came out to support us multiple times.

Personally, I would like to thank Mallory Dimmitt, Joe Guthrie and Elam Stoltzfus for their multiple-year commitment to this cause, leadership before, during and since the expedition, friendship and contributions to this book. This book was shaped by Lisa Baylor's keen eye and Hannah Dillard's brilliant design. I thank them for their dedication and long hours. Hilary Swain, Tom Hoctor, Mallory, Joe, my parents and wife really came through to help edit the text. I also thank Barbara O'Reilley, editor of FORUM Magazine, for giving me the impetus to start writing this story.

My brother, Travis Ward, joined the trek more than any other, always making it better for us all. My wife Suzie deserves special thanks for supporting my multi-year focus on the expedition and multi-month absence during our first years of marriage, plus her 43-mile mountain bike performance when she joined us for a day in Big Cypress.

Last but not least, I offer great personal gratitude to the ranchers and agricultural landowners, many friends who I met during the course of documenting Florida ranches in previous years, who welcomed the team to visit their lands during the expedition. Florida ranchers, farmers, foresters, biologists and public land managers are my heroes for what they do to keep our natural heritage alive.

28°41'37" N 81°2'21" W Econlockhatchee River (photo by Joe Guthrie)